BAB I

Introduction

I.1. Background Issues

It has been 60 years of free Indonesia, but efforts to educate people's lives in particular and the nation in general seem as if the road is in place. On the one part, education software, including the education system and the quality of human resources and teachers and managers, is still stuck in patchy policies. On the other hand, educational facilities and infrastructure are far from adequate because the budget of education costs is very low. As a result, the accessibility of children in this country towards a very low quality education. Meanwhile, the quality of learning in general does not improve because the welfare of teachers does not improve.

Walhasil, the practice of commercialization of education, turned out to be cultured. Many schools start to charge for education that seems unaffordable to the public. For the able it doesn't seem to matter. But what about students whose family's economic level is still low or below welfare standards? Finally the story of students who try to kill themselves for reasons of not being able to pay SPP becomes news that often adorns the mass media. Not to mention the news of the collapse of school buildings is adding to the excitement of our education world at this time. There is still an education organization utilizing shady houses or trees for teaching and learning activities. Not designed so, but because of the lack of facilities available.

The publication of reform rays in all fields post-1998 participated in illuminating the natural thinking of the world of education in Indonesia which was previously in dimness. This is possible because education is not a self-contained entity but rather is related to reciprocity with social, economic, political, even legal and security philosophies and systems. Education is indeed an extraordinarily dense area and the elements are in number. The complexity of education reflects the complexity of national and state life. Thus any change in the educational torso indicates a change in almost all fields.[1]

Chairman of the General Board (PB) of the Teachers Association of the Republic of Indonesia (PGRI) Sulistiyo said that education is threatened bychronic problems that are very worrying with the renewal of lesseffective, efficienteducation. PGRI hopes that this education issue should be a serious concern by making diknas the main national agenda. "Education is now very worrying, so it should be a serious concern as the main national agenda,"he said at the Umum Hearing Meeting (RDPU) Special Committee (Pansus) Education of the Regional Representative Council (DPD) on the 2nd

---

[1] Kh. Abdullah Syukri Zarkasyi, But *Pesantren Management Modern Pondok Gontor Experience*, (Print II; Gontor: Trimurti Press, 2005), p. 2.

floor of the DPD Building parliament complex, Senayan-Jakarta, led by its chairman, Sudharto.

The chronicproblem of education stems from the indifference or ignorance of state organizers about the role of education for the development and progress of the nation in the future. Because it is displayed to the extent of schooling or eradicating illiteracy, education is threatened by chronic problems. "In fact, the cumulative effect of success in education ismarwah or self-esteem," he said. Sulistiyo exposes the chronic problems that the new administration must address. One, in the fundamental realm, the philosophy of education has not answered the national goal of smarting about life mandated the Opening of the Constitution of the Republic of Indonesia year 1945. "It shouldbe widespread," he said. The expansion of intelligence includes intelligence quotient (IQ) , emotional quotient (EQ) , and spiritual quotient (SQ) known as multiple intelligence (MI). All of which reinforces the notionthat kecerdasan transcends intelligence. According to him, the blurring of the paradigm leads to the inaccuracy of the target (mismatch) of the implementation of education to the needs and problems of society.

Generally, graduates of the education unit do not have the qualification conformity and spiritual mental readiness, such as reasoning and ethos, skills, entrepreneurship, and leadership. It is ironic, Sulistiyo for example, faculty alumni / agriculture majors are not interested in working in agriculture, so the agricultural sector languish in this agrarian country and we instead import agriculturalkomoditi. Thefaculty /marine department is also so. "We are late to promote marine studies in this archipelago. As a result, the marine sector remains languishing and we are instead stealing many marine commodities. Later, the faculty/department of agriculture and marine in the college was not in demand calon students," he said. [2]That is a glimpse into the condition of Indonesian education today. In the midst of the national education system, pondok pesantren appears as an Islamic educational institution that began to be looked at by many circles. Because boarding schools have been successful in printing cadres of people, scholars, and leaders both at the local and national level. Even pesantren continues to grow and work to play its function and role in all areas of life.

Talking about pesantren or boarding school as an Islamic educational institution is very important and interesting, especially for educational practitioners and community leaders. By knowing pesantren education we know the role, function, and contribution of boarding schools as educational institutions and Islamic da'wah in realizing civil society in Indonesia.

---

[2] http://www.satunews.com/read/3383/2009/06/26/pgri--kondisi-pendidikan-nasio-html

Pondok pesantren as a permanent educational institution istiqamah and consistently performs its role as a center of deepening religious sciences (*tafaquh fi al-din*)and Islamic da'wah institutions as well as participating in the smartening of the nation has been recognized by the community, evidenced by its successin printing religious figures, nation fighters and public figures, whether in the pre-independence period, after independence or in this day and age. This is a clear proof that boarding schools have contributed a lot in building the Nation of Indonesia.[3]

Pondok pesantren education is the oldest education system in Indonesia, which has characteristics and has produced major scholars and national figures. The development of the times gave birth to changes in society while changing the pattern and education system of pesantren, the origin does not change the orientasi and the values of pesantren.

I. 2. Problem Formulation

Departing from the background above, the author formulates two points of concern that will be discussed in this paper, namely:

1. What are the prospects and possibilities of boarding schools to be encouraged to become ideal Islamic educational

---

[3] KH. Abdullah Syukri Zarkasyi, MA, *Gontor and Pesantren Education Renewal*, (Jakarta: PT. RajaGrafindo Persada,2005), p.1.

institutions and as the   center of the development of Indonesian Muslim civilization in the future?

2. What challenges will boarding schools face in the future?

3. What elements can encourage modern islamic boarding schools to become ideal Islamic educational institutions and central to the development of Indonesian Muslim civilization in the future?

I. 3. Research Objectives

The research in this paper aims to answer the questions in the formulation of problems that are to:

1. Knowing the prospect of modern boarding schools as an ideal Islamic educational institution in the future that will be datag so as to make it possible to be the center of the development of Muslim civilization in Indonesia..

2. Knowing the challenges that boarding schools will face in the future amidst the current globalization and the development of the times.

3. Knowing the important elements that can drive modern boarding schools into an Ideal Islamic educational institution that serves as the center of the development of Muslim civilization in Indonesia.

Discussion

Education is one of the areas*of concern of* Muslim thinkers and activists throughout the Islamic world. Thinkers and activists of the movement, such as Muh. Abduh in Egypt and Sayyid Ahmad Khan in the Indian Subcontinent made education the main agenda of the Islamist movement they were able to support. The thinkers and activists not only established Islamic educational institutions, they also sought to transform traditional educational institutions into modern educational institutions. In the Indian Subcontinent, Sayyid Ahmad Khan founded Alighar University which fully adopted oxford university's education system. While in Egypt, Muhammad Abduh tried to transform modern sciences into Azhar University. It can be said that from the beginning of the 19th century to the beginning of the 20th century almost the entire Islamic world witnessed the establishment of modern educational institutions.

II.1. A Brief History and Definition of Boarding School

The growth of pesantren started from the condition of*an* 'alim who tinggal in a certain area who then came students who thenstudied to him. Over time the alim residence was insufficient until the students together built a lodger so that many buildings were erected around the kyai house. The longer the buildings developed so that it became a cottage area as the residence of the students, which eventually became known by the name of pondok or pesantren.

In Java the place of religious teaching is known by the name of pesantren or pondok. The term cottage actually comes from Arabic funduq which means hotel or hostel. [4]The term pesantren means place to ride the students.. [5]There is no meaningful difference between the designation of cottage and pesantrend, as both refer to the same meaning. The name Pondok Tebuireng, Pondok Termas, Pondok Krapyak or Pesantren Tebuireng, Pesantren Termas, Pesantren Krapyak does not show any difference in meaning. Therefore in this paper, the term pesantren is used as a synonym of the word pondok or used at the same time as not being a boarding school.

The boarding school is usually interpreted as an educational institution and islamic teaching, umunya in a non-classical way, where a kyai teaches Islam to students based on books written in Arabic by medieval Arabic scholars, the students usually live in huts (dormitories) in the boarding school.[6]

------

[4] K.H. Imam Zarkasyi, *Introductory Week Book Part II,* (Gontor: Darussalam Press).

[5] K.H. Abdullah Syukri Zarkasyi, MA, *Op. Cit*, p. 2.

[6] Tim LP3ES, *Pesantren Profile* (Jakarta: LP3ES, 1975), p. 6.

According to Yacub, pesantren means an Islamic educational institution that is generally in a non-classical way, the teacher is a man who has islamic knowledge through classical religious books (yellow book) with Arabic writing in ancient Malay or in Arabic, the books are usually thework of Islamic scholars (Arabic) in medieval times.[7]

Zamakhsyari Dofier mentions that pesantren consists of five main elements, namely; kyai, students, mosques, huts, and the teaching of classical Islamic books. [8]These five elements are a special feature that pesantren has and distinguish the education of boarding schools with other forms of educational institutions. Although these five elements support each other's existence of a peasntren but kyai plays such a central role in the world of pesantren. Because kyai is the central figure in a boarding school. While (the late) K.H. Imam Zarkasyi defined boarding school as an Islamic educational institution with a dormitory or cottage system, where kyai as the central figure, the mosque as the center of activities that animate it, and the teaching of Islam under the guidance of kyai as its utam activity.[9]

---

[7] Muhammad Yacub, *Boarding School and Village Community Development*, (Bandung: Angkasa, 1993), p. 65.

[8] Zamakhsyari Dofier, *Pesantren Tradition: The Study of Kyai's Life View* (Jakarta: LP3ES, 1984), p. 19.

[9] Kh. Imam Zarkasyi, *Introductory Week*, Part II.

The definition of boarding school according to K.H. Imam zarkasyi is more complete and comprehensive, because it has advantages than other definitions. First, pesantren must be a full residential Islamic boarding school. Second, kyai function as central figure (uswah hasanah), who plays the role of teacher (mu'alim), educator (murabbi), and mentor (mursyid). Third, the mosque as the center of activity, and the Fourth, the material taught is not limited to the yellow book only.

Judging by its origins, pesantren has very strong tradis roots in Indonesian society because pesantren merupaka one of the symbols of indonesian education culture (nusatara). Historically the islamic education system is rooted in religious educational traditions as Hinduism and Buddhism flourished in Indonesia. Since the beginning of the 13th century, islamization that took place in the Archipelago has transformed the culture of education into a form of boarding school. In this case, the Islamization of the Archipelago provides a new content of the Islamic version of the Hindu and Buddhist religious education system. That is why in terms of name, "peantren" according to C.C. Berg as quoted by Dofier, is often associated with the Indian term shastri which means people know hindu scriptures or people who are experts on scripture.[10]

---

[10] Dofier, *Tradition*, p. 18.

The term santri is also associated with the Tamil word "sattiri" which means "a person living in a poor house orbuilding into agamaan in general. [11]Santri in ancient times is different from santri in this day and age. Along with the development of the times, the boarding school also equips its students with various skills such as computers, scouts, speech training, scouting, and other extracurricular activities that support educational and teaching skills that are in accordance with the demands of the times.

II. 2. Boarding School Education Orientation

Pesantren is an independent educational institution that was pioneered, managed, and developed by kyai. If traced pesantren is born from something very simple. A person known to have religious knowledge, which is then considered ustadz, prepares to teach Islam. From simple things about the basics of Islamic teaching knowledge, such as how to read the Qur'an, to deeper knowledge, such as how to understand the Qur'an, interpretation, hadith, fiqh, Sufism, and other similar knowledge.

At first pesantren developedsimply. However, becauseof the spirit, earnestness and continuous hard work   and learning system developed oriented towards the community based education

---

[11] Ministry of Religious Affairs, *History of Madrasah Development,* (Jakarta: Directorate General of Institutional Development of Islamic Religion, 1999), p. 95.

then in the course of some boarding schools became a large Islamic educational institution. The number of students studying is growing, the institution managed is called boarding school, and the leadership holder of the institution is called kyai. Boarding schools are always equipped with mosques (mushalla) and kyai houses. Students learn religion by living and hanging out with kyai.

Para observers of boarding schools identify pesantren with some characteristics that in pesantren there are kyai houses, mosques, and santri housing. The students learned to do and practice what kyai did. The relationship between santri and kyai resembles a father-son relationship. Kyai not only teaches religious science, but also guides, exemplifies or exemplifies, and "prays" for his students. Their relationship s delved into various aspects of life, both rational, emotional, and spiritual aspects in depth. Kyai enacts her students like their own children by sharing compassion and making herself an ideal role model.

The illustration above provides an overview of the comparison of boarding schools with modern educational institutions in general, in the form of schools or universities. In schools and universities, private teachers and lecturers must melt into institutional power. Through such conceptual frameworks, students and students study into institutions or institutions, and not to personal institutions. Therefore, if in pesantren kyai is central and a symbol of solid strength, then in modern educational institutions (schools and universities) the main strength is in its insitution.[12]

Following the development of recent times pesantren has opened up. If the boarding school used to be just a place to practice religious science through the sorogan, wetonan, and bandongan systems, then today it has opened up the education of classical systems and even new modern and formal-faced programs such as madrassas, schools, and even universities. Even if modern education has entered pesantren, it should not shift its tradition, namely the style of boarding school. On the other hand, the presence of formal educational institutions into pesantren is intended to strengthen the existing tradition, namely boarding school model education. This is an inevitability without omitting the characteristics of pesantren (al-muhâfazhah' ala al-qadîm as-shâlih wa al-akhdzu bi al-jadîd al-ashlah).

The tradition that is meant to always be maintained by pesantren is the teaching of religion in its entirety. Boarding school education from the beginning is not intended to prepare a skilled workforce in modern sectors as schools and universities generally wish. Instead it is oriented to how students can understand, live, and practice Islamic teachings well. Pesantren education is an

[12] Prof. Dr. H. Imam Suprayogo, *Ibid*, http://rektor.uin-malang.ac.id

Islamic education that seeks to bring students into alim and shalih, not to be employees or officials. Therefore, some boarding schools that are still "pure" do not prioritize diplomas or certificates, but rather on the mastery of science as a provision of life guidance. The orientation of boarding school education that implies students can/may leave pesantren if they have felt enough. On the contrary, a dozen and decades of students are "allowed" to study in pesantren and even from one boarding school to another to increase their religious knowledge while feeling insufficient.

Such educational orientation makes in pesantren not knowing or known a student minister, let alone forealizing the list of grades, diplomas, and making programs that are oriented towards the formal aspect by abandoning the substantial aspect. It is rational that pesantren does not know the distant class program and executive class (Saturday-Sunday) which is feared to damage the quality of education. In addition, pesantren is rich in education system decorated by the values of sincerity, ridha, tawadhu', karamah, barakah, and the like. Here lies the difference between boarding school education and modern education (schools and universities). Admittedly or not, not a few figures, both local and national levels, are born from boarding schools. Prof. H.A. Mukti Ali, a former Minister of Religion, once stated that "pesantren ya pesantren and there have never been any scholars born from institutions other than pesantren." What Prof. H.A. Mukti Ali says is the fact that Indonesian scholars are mostly or even entirely born from boarding schools.

Today, there is an effort to update the islamic education system by opening formal educational institutions, ranging from basic level (MI/SD Islam), middle level (MTs./SMP Islam and MA/SMA Islam), to PTAI and Islamic universities. The characteristic of an independent and autonomous boarding school with kyai as an orientation center, makes pesantren still exist and even seen as an alternative education system. The key to self-reliance and the robustness of pesantren is in kyai. If the boarding school is strong enough, then it will move forward. In East Java, for example, Pondok Pesantren Modern Gontor, Ponorogo; Al-Amien Prenduan Boarding School, Sumenep; Pondok Pesantren Salafiyah-Shafi'iyah Asem Bagus, Situbondo; Sidogiri Boarding School, Pasuruan; Pondok Pesantren Karang Asem Paciran, Lamongan (touted as a boarding school affiliated with Muhammadiyah); and many more are progressing and notoriety.

Getting here, I think it's naïve to have one or a group of people downplaying the meaning of boarding school. It is conceivable that pesantren conoacting as a traditional education remains solid amid the struggles of the system and the increasing education model. Not only that, pesantren is the only institution that successfully transmits Islam and even for the progress of this

Indonesian nation. Because the glory of pesantren lies in not only the orientation of the material but its existence is more oriented to the enrichment of knowledge and nobility of the mind. It is not wrong that pesantren is said to be the bodyguard of the enactment of "jihad based management", as it is currently bubbling.

Efforts towards advancing pesantren are now being pursued. Like the equalization of the managed education system, the recognition of diplomas issued, and even the recognition of graduates of pesantren is equivalent to modern education (schools and universities). Law No. 20 of 2003 on the National Education System is evidence for a glimmer of the struggle of pesantren to stand in line with the modern education system. Although in some areas found pesantren to maintain its tradition and identity without following the formal provisions of the government.

II. 3. Boarding School Education Methodology

The word method comes from the Greek, namely metha (through or passing) and hodos (way or way). While according to the General Dictionary of Bahasa Indonesia method is a systemal way of working to facilitate the delivery of an activity in order to achieve the goals that have been announced. So the method of education is a way or way taken by educators (in this case kyai and its caregivers) in the activities of educational activities found in pesantren educational institutions.[13]

While according to the term method adlah a certain way (specific) appropriate to present an educational material, so as to achieve the purpose of education, either in the form of short-term goals or long-term goals, where students can receive education and teaching easily and be able to capture the meaning contained in it and in the end the students can practice educational materials without any element of coercion (emphasis).

The method of education in pesantren educational institutions (in the teaching of yellow book in general) according to Mastuhu there are four, *namely: sorogan, bandongan, halaqoh, dan and memorization..* [14]While Imran Arifin mentions four types of educational methods, namely *badongan, sorogan, muhawarah,*and *mudzakarah.*

The Sorogan method is a method of educational or teaching form that is individual, in which the students one by one come to the kyai or its helpers by carrying a particular book. Then kyai or his helper read the book a few lines with the meaning (meaning) that is prevalent in pesantren (usually in Javanese). After kyai or his helpers have finished reading the book, the students repeat it, after which it is considered sufficient, then the other students advance in turn.

---

[13] K.H. Abdullah Syukri, *Op. Cit.*, p. 72.

[14] Mastuhu, *Dynamics of Pesantren Education System* (Jakarta: INIS, 1994), p. 61.

This method of sorogan according to Imran Arifin, is a form of method that is considered complicated. This is because the method requires patience, craft, and discipline personally. This means that success in this method is predominantly determined by the strictness of the santri against kyai and its embrace, although in fact the explanation of the kyai or its helpers also determines. And usually this method takes precedence for novice students, but there are also special students who want to study certain books.[15]

The *wetonan method* is a way of learning in groups followed by students and usually kyai (his helpers) using a regional language that directly translates it sentence by sentence from the book he studied. Menururt Prasodjo, this method is thought to mimic the mdel of Mecca, which is the habit of glorifying in the Masjid Al-Haram, where a sheikh recites and explains a book and is swarmed by a number of his disciples with each holding the same book, who[16] diligently listens to and records the sheikh's description, both done directly on the sheets of his book mauun on the other sheet of paper.

Halaqoh method is a method similar to bandongan, only in this method there is a discussion to understand the content of the book, and the discussion is done not to question the possibility of right or wrong

---

[15] Imran Arifin, *Kyai Leadership, Tebuireng Boarding School Case,* (Jombang: Kalimasada Press, 1991), p. 38.

[16] Sadiq Khan, *Pesantren Profile,* (Jakarta: LP3ES, 1975), p. 53.

what is taught by kyai (his helpers), but only to understand what the intent or meaning is taught by kyai or his helpers.

The method of hapalan is a way of studying the contents of the book that has been learned from kyai by memorizing, where students are required to memorize a chapter of (a lesson) to be listened to to kyai (his helpers).

Muhawarah method is an activity that trains to speak (communicate) using Arabic required by kyai to students as long as they settle in boarding school institutions. [17]In some pesantren this method is not required every day but only once a week or there are also two maynggu. There are even those who are joined at the time of conducting arabic speech practice activities, which are basically aimed at practicing the skills of students speaking in Arabic. So students have a mental readiness to speak in front of crowds.

II. 4. Education Curriculum of Pondok Pesantren

The term curriculum comes from the French language,*namely "courir"*which *means to run,*meaning to run. While in Greek the curriculum is defined as "distance" that must be taken by runners, so the curriculum in education is interpreted as a number of

---

[17] Arifin *Kyai's leadership*, p. 32.

lessons that must be taken or [18]completed by the protégé in case of obtaining a diploma.[19]

The word curriculum began to be known as a term in the world of education more or less a century ago. The term appeared for the first time in webster dictionaries in 1856. In that year the word curriculum was used in the field of sports, which is a tool that takes people from the start to the finish line. It was not until about 1955 that the term curriculum was used in the field of education with the meaning of a number of subjects in an educational institution.

In webster dictionary the curriculum has two kinds of understandings that are almost the same:

1. A number of subjects that students must take or study at a school or college institution in order to obtain a diploma.
2. A number of subjects are offered by an educational institution or a study.

---

[18] H.M. Arifin, *Philosophy of Islamic Education*, (Jakarta: Bina Aksara, 1987), p. 84.

[19] Nana Sudjana, *Coaching and Curriculum Development in Schools,* (Bandung: Sinar Baru, 1991), p. 4.

From some of the above, it can be understood that what is meant by the curriculum is something that must be taken by students in completing a program.

While in islamic education studies the term curriculum uses the word "manhaj" which means as a bright path or a path that is passed by man in various areas of his life. The path of light is the path that educators and mentors go through with educated or guided people in order to develop their skills and attitudes. [20] In addition, Addamardasy Sarhan and Munir Kamil interpret the curriculum as " a number of educational experiences.[21]

In some educational institutions pesantren is not announced in detail the unit of teaching program. This is because the program belongs to the absolute character of a kyai, so the desired specific target is less clear. For example, in a year's time students must understand a particular book. This means students have the freedom to understand a book without being limited by age or target time.

Although on the one hand this model is similar to the democratic system of teaching that is being discourse today, on

---

[20] Omar Muhammad al-Taumy al-Syaibany, *Philosophy of Education*, Pen. Hasan Langgulung, p.478.

[21] al-Syaibany, *Philosophy of Education*, p. 478.

the other hand has weaknesses and can lead to program delays in the teaching process while the most severe impact is the delay for students who are less disciplined using time, because they tend to relax uncontrolled with the target time and age.

In traditional pesantren education institutions (salaf) curriculum (teaching materials) varies greatly, because the curriculum in the pesantren model is very determined by the manager of the institution (kyai). But in general, teaching in salaf boarding schools is classical books especially by scholars who adhere to Shafi'iyah which is the only teaching material given in the lemabaga environment of pesantren at that time. In subsequent developments, many pesantren institutions that have taught general sciences that are considered not to deviate from their main purpose, namely educating prospective scholars who remain consistent on islamic teachings.

At this time, the books taught in some boarding schools are starting to vary, even though the boarding school does not or has not used the classical form or used the national curriculum. However, in fact, the institutions began to try to make changes to the curriculum based on the educational personnel available to the institution.

Pondok Pesntren Modern has generally combined the teaching of religious sciences and general sciences, so there is no dichotomy of science in modern boarding schools. In addition to being equipped with religious and general knowledge they are also equipped with a variety of life skills including, scouting, organizing, speech training, discussion exercises and various other extracurricular activities that support the formation of their character and character.

II. 5. Characteristics and Characteristics of Modern Boarding School

Pesantren as the oldest and original Islamic educational institution of Indonesia has made a great role in participating in the intelligent life of people and nations. In the past pesantren was a very reliable HR Bank. From Pesantren was born public figures, alim scholars, clever clever, and leaders of the nation. This is an indisputable historical fact. As an educational institution, pesantren has a special place in the hearts of the community. This may be because of three things: 1) because pesantren is the oldest educational institution in the country. The age of pesantren is almost the same as the age of the coming of Is;am itself to Indonesia, 2) pesantren represents, even identical to the meaning of Islam itself, 3) pesantren, as *observers often point out, is indigenous* i.e. native (typical) Nusantra which is not found in other places, including in the Middle East.[22]

The characteristics of modernity pesantren can be seen from several aspects, among others: *Petrama,* institutional aspects, management and organization of pesantren. Pesantren modern is an educational institution that is converted. Through this appansanit, boarding school ownership has gone from private or family property to public property. *Second, the* education system aspect. Modern pesantren combines a boarding system that has the advantage of dormitory system and planting pattern of religious values and strong mental *attitude* formation with madrasah/school system that has excellence in the field of methodology and management of learning. *Third, the* curriculum aspect. The modern boarding school curriculum does not dichotomy between religious sciences and general sciences. These two scientific fields are integrated into a whole unit of scientific epistimology buildings that are all of religious value. Similarly, in the modern pesantren curriculum is not separated between the field of intracurricular activities and the ectracurricular, both are integrated into the entire total activity of pesantren so that both get the same attention. Both form an environment with various activities within it that are all intended for educational purposes. *Fourth, the* learning system aspect. Modern pesantren organizes learning activities with a

---

[22] DR. H. Baharudin, HS, MA, *Reform and Modernization of Islamic Education in Indonesia Pesantren World Perspective*, Paper (http://www.pmiicamar.com).

classical system. Learning activities for all subject matter are classically implemented with a planned and measured system of administration, supervision, and evaluation. *Fifth, the* learning method aspect. The formal learning method used is one that allows a student or learner to learn more effectively and efficiently by actively engaging them in the learning process. Learning methods that focus on dialogue, questioning, discussion, demonstrations, exercises, assignments, and the like become important in an effort to create a conducive learning atmosphere. *Sixth, the* infrastructure aspect. Modern boarding school education is equipped with infrastructure that supports its success which at least includes mosques, dormitories, libraries, study rooms, laboratories, teacher housing, offices, auditoriums, and sports facilities.

The education curriculum in pesantren has a vision and mission that leads to the achievement efforts of the student figure who wants to be born by pesantren. Therefore, the cult character of pesantren combines all elements of santri proficiency both intellectual, emotional, and spiritual. This also means that the boarding school curriculum is not only cognitive, but combines the entire realm of learner self-development, whether cognitive, affective, or psychomotor. Because education dominated by cognitive concentration alone will result in pragmatic humans. Children will only be profit-oriented without consideration of values and ethics, especially when the evaluation of education only concerns cognitive mastery (remember the recent UN results). Because such conditions only consume the concentration of children, teachers, and schools in pursuit of assessment targets.

Zamakhsyari Dhofier as quoted by Ridlwan Nasir states that Pondok Pesantren has special characteristics that distinguish it from other educational institutions, namely:[23]

1. The absence of Kyai (Abuya, Mr., Ajengan, or Tuan Guru) as the central figure is usually also called the owner.
2. There is a dormitory as the residence of the students, where the mosque is the center.
3. The education and teaching of Religion through the system of study (weton, serogan, bendongan).
4. So in general pesantren must consist of a minimum of Kyai, Santri, Masjid, Dormitory / cottage, and the study of books (usually in the form of yellow books).

According to Mastuhu there are several principles that apply to education ordered trends that describe the main characteristics of pesantren:[24]

---

[23] http://www.stail.ac.id, *Boarding School between Modernization and The Khithah*, Makakalah.

[24] Ibid, Paper

1. Have wisdom according to islamic teachings. Students are helped to understand the meaning of life, as well as its responsibilities in society.

2. Have a led freedom. That is, freedom is based on god who determines everything, man only strives with his creativity.

3. Independence. Both students and pesantren have a soul of self-reliance in their lives, so that the students do not cry, and develop into a resilient person and do not give up easily.

4. It has a high togetherness. Their lives, which are always together in the same circumstances, result in the ingrained good togetherness between students, ustadz, and kyai.

5. High respect for Master. This is in contrast if we look at the state of Public schools for example that some of their students have no respect for people who have been able to guide and help them become useful human beings.

6. Simplicity. This simple attitude is what animates pesantren so that it exists until now. Simple is not synonymous with poverty, but it is more about putting things in proportion.

The character that distinguishes Pesantren from other educational institutions is that Pesantren as an Educational Institution also plays the role of religious guidance institution, scientific, training, community mining, and at the same time becoming a cultural node. So as to form a willing and able people to work in the community. Because it has a sense of moral responsibility to develop what has been learned and obtained from boarding schools that have educated and guided it.

II. 6. Consistency of Pesantren's Role in Education

Until now, podok pesantren still remains istiqamah, and consistently performs its role as a deepening center of religious sciences and islamic da'wah institutions. The alumni of boarding schools who are competent and have the ability, have a moral obligation to establish a new boarding school, with an educational model that has been experienced or with little modification.

The question is what keeps boarding schools and consistently performs its role? Broadly, there are three things that contain boarding schools that remain istiqamah and consistent namely:[25]

1. The Value and Soul of Boarding School

The first aspect is the islamic and educational values found in boarding schools. The fact that boarding school actually lies in the values of the cottage reflected in the spirit of the cottage itself. It is this value that will determine the philosophy of life. The soul of this boarding school can differ from one boarding school and another. In Pondok Modern

---

[25] K.H. Abdullah Syukri Zarkasyi, MA, *Op. Cit* Foreword to The Leader of Modern Hut Gontor, p. X.

Darussalam Gontor for example, there are five popular values known as "Panca Jiwa Pondok" namely sincerity, simplicity, dikari or self-reliance, Islamic ukhuwah, and freedom. It is this soul that ensures the survival of boarding schools, and without this soul pesantren will lose its identity despite being able to adopt various systems and educational materials that are always insanity with the times. Like man, this soul is his spirit, like deeds, this soul is the intention and weight of his sincerity, and like prayer, the soul is his kekhusuka.

2. **Dormitory System**

The second aspect is a dormitory system full of discipline. This boarding system supports the creation of integrated education centers; school education (formal), family education (informal), and community education (nonformal). In pesantren life the three elements can be combined. Their families are nannies, teachers, and fellow students. Their school is on a campus run by the boarding school's own people, and their community is a santri community.

This boarding system strongly supports the implementation of the curriculum for twenty-four hours. Therefore, integrated education centers have advantages compared to non-pesantren in the following terms. First, efficient coordination capabilities because all functionaries are on campus. Second, the ability to form and care for students from environmental influences by utilizing what is in the cottage as a means of education. Third, there is a mosque that serves as the center of animating activities, as well as kyai as the central figure.

3. **Boarding school education**materials.

The third aspect is the material. The materials taught in boarding schools represent the existing curriculum. Namely the curriculum that is a combination of religious science (revealed knowlege) and kawniyah science (aquired knowlege). So in pesantren there has been the integration of science. In other terms there is no scientific dualism in the world of education.

Keep in mind that from the above three aspects, pesantren education systems and materials can be changed and updated according to the situation and conditions, demands of society, and the progress of the times. However, the islamic values in pesantren should not change because it dimmed the morality order that is rahmatan lil'alamin (universal) based on the Qur'an and Hadith.

By paying attention to these three aspects (values, systems and materials), pondok pesantren as the oldest educational institution in Indonesia plays a very vital role in preparing civil society through modernization of pesantren education system. With modernization pesantren is expected to be able to form and produce human resources (HR) that have a holistic personality (human kamil). That is a personality that has a balance between five aspects: spiritul, intellectual, social, emotional and physical.

The kamil individual is not formed instantly, but requires a fairly long process. This process is *a transfer of knowlege and education of moral values from one generation to another genaeration.* With another sense is the transfer of science and the planting of moral values (Islam) from one generation to another, this is the essence of peasntren education. In order for this process to take place effectively and efficiently, a conducive educational environment, an integrative andcomprehensive curriculum, a dynamic academic atmosphere, professional teaching staff, adequate learning support facilities, and more importantly*conditioning*through the example of educators inboarding schools.

II. 6.1. The Strategic Role of Boarding School

Today pondokpesantren is the center of all forms of Life of Muslims. Not only being a place of learning that is indeed the main function of pesantren but more than that, pesantren has developed into an economic, social, pilitik, kemasyarkatan and community empowerment center. From the past until now pesantren does have a very strategic role.

1. **Era of the Kingdom or Sultanate of Islam in Indonesia (1450-1650)**

   The long history of pesantren began when Raden Patah (a chinese msulim) who was the Wali Songo (some of whom are said to be Muslims of Chinese descent and all of whom are leaders of the great boarding school) succeeded in shifting majapahit kingdom and established demak Islamic work around the xv abab, thus endingthe Hindu/Buddhist kingdoms in Indonesia that had begun from the second century as well as abab XV AD.

   In this period pesantren serves as the center of the change of the community, which is carried out through the spread of Islam and the political role that influences the kings and the casting of Java in trade activities and the opening of new areas.

2. **Dutch and Japanese Colonial Period (1650-1945)**

   When the Dutch with the Political divide et empera had a problem with the kingdoms in Indonesia, pesantren acted as a center of defense and resistance to the dutch invaders.

3. **Era of The Revolution of The Independence and Old Order (1945-1965)..**

When the Tebuireng boarding school under K.H. Wahid Hasyim became the front line of Hezbollah-Sabilillah, pesantren took on the role of "revolutionary force".

4. **Zaman Orde Baru (1967-1999)**

The Government of the Indoensia Republic of The Era of President Suharto and Habibie viewed pesantren as "development potential" and had a significant political role in terms of the number of approximately 8,749 boarding schools with the number of students approximately 2 million people, as well as its figures who played a role in the Order of Reform such as Wahid, Cak Nur, Cak Nun, and others.

5. **Reformation period to date (1999-2010)**

In this time, the alumni of pesantren boarding school have worked and played a role in all life lines. Start the world of business, education, politics and security defense. To be a leader who is in the community both at the local and national level.

II. 6.2. Pesantren as Formal Education Complement

It should be acknowledged that not all boarding schools have been properly maintained, as it is also the case that not all formal educational institutions are running as they should. However, lately it has become increasingly recognized that pesantren holds forces that are not owned by formal educational institutions. The relationship between kyai and students who wake up solidly, so that kyai's role is not limited as a teacher, but also as a pamong, mentor, caregiver, educator and even make students like their own children, is an atmosphere that should be developed in the educational process anywhere including in a formal educational institution. Formal and even transactional relationships do not occur in boarding schools. Kyai and students by being in one place equipped with mosques, libraries and other facilities, then the real educational values are more likely to be implemented.

More than that, many aspects of educational success are achieved by pesantren and not so by public schools. For example, not a few universities still fail to develop foreign language skills, --Arabic and English, but it turns out that gontor ponorogo boarding school, Al-Amien Perinduan Sumenep Madura, which is in the countryside, turned out to be successful. It is ironic that public education and even including many universities in big cities still have not managed to catch up with the progress of some of these boarding schools. In addition, the alumni of boarding schools are not the few who are able to do leadership, especially in religious life in the community, even if they are without a bachelor's degree. Meanwhile, college alumni who have been equipped with long degrees, it turns out that do not find a job for others, while to meet the needs of themselves there is still a lot of confusion.

Seeing the advantages of pesantren tradition, not least now formal educational institutions are formatted into a synesa between public education and pesantren and even Prof. A.Malik Fadjar, M.Sc former Minister of Religion and Minister of Education once wrote a book on Sintesa Higher Education and Pesantren as an Effort to Present Alternative Educational Institutions. No less, the idea has been implemented at The Islamic State University (UIN) Malang. Since ten years ago, UIN Malang formatted Islamic educational institutions with a form of synesth between pesantren and university. In the first and second years ----for a while, adjusting the facilities available, the University requires all new students to be housed in Ma'had Al Aly Sunan Ampel. After the program lasted approximately ten years, it turned out to bring results. If there have previously been complaints about weak students in Arabic and English, it turns out that by presenting the tradition of boarding schools on campus, that weakness has been a little overcome. Similarly, with those residing in Ma'had, religious traditions can be built more intensively, for example getting used to students praying in prayer at five times, reading the Qur'an and others. In addition, the relationship between lecturers and students, even if not exactly, has been spared the transactional and formal nuances. Lately with the campus pesantren appears symptoms, began to appear new phenomena such as memorizing activities of the Qur'an. Not a few students from majors ---physics, chemistry, biology, mathematics, engineering, economics who participated in this activity. Apparently this kind of educational format is an attraction for the community and therefore lately, according to some information, will be developed by several other Islamic universities.

Looking at such facts, then in the development of education in Indonesia whose society is very compound, and is in the midst of such a rapid change, it is necessary to find alternatives as an effort to improve the quality of education that is able to answer the challenges of the times. I see the serious issue of this education implementation not in who the organizer is and what it looks like, but on its commitment to efforts to improve the quality of the results. Lately there has been a boarding school, which is called traditional it turns out to have entered the modern category and instead appears an educational institution called modern when in fact very retarded, in the sense of not adjusting to its times. The last mentioned institution ignores quality and even organizes programs that are very far from the demands of minimum requirements, the implementation is simply a formality whose activities are no more dividing the diploma easily, without visiting a reasonable process. Therefore, the key word in improving education is how we build a shared commitment to make educational institutions more thoroughly qualified, both in the public education environment and in pesantren. Apparently the synesa between public education and pesantren is an alternative to reducing each other's weaknesses, especially in the face of challenges and future HR preparation. Allahu a'lam.

II. 7. Boarding Schools and Future Islamic Education Formats

Boarding schools were originally identified as "village symptoms." The symptoms of the village mean that boarding schools are traditional Islamic educational institutions whose presence is not to prepare for the fulfillment of skilled or professional labor as the demands of modern society today. Boarding school was founded by individuals, namely kyai. This educational institution is intended to teach students to learn religion from the basic to the advanced level. Kyai is the main center of the establishment of boarding school. There has never been a boarding school without kyai. The authority of pesantren leadership is entirely at the end of the day. Therefore, the existence and development of pesantren is determined by the strength of kyai in question. If kyai dies, it will be automatically passed on by the descendants or close family of the kyai concerned. Lately in pesantren built organizations like modern educational institutions. However, apparently, kyai still holds the authority of all things related to his boarding school life. So strong is the strength of kyai in each pesantren, so that large organizations such as NU known as the kyai organization, are not very powerful to take part in controlling pesantren. Alternatively, pesantren does not require intervention from external circles such as NU or moreover the government. It is a symptom of the new, lately islamic boarding school seen by the wider community, no exception oraganization of Islam that claims to be a modernist movement, namely Muhammadiyah. Muhammadiyah is better known as an Islamic organization that has established and developed many schools, lately it has begun to see how important pesantren educational institutions are. Only Muhammadiyah so far does not have much kyai. Because kyai is mostly born from pesantren. Muhammadiyah, meanwhile, emphasizes the development of school education models, giving birth to more teachers, lecturers, employees, and the like. I rate, the phenomenon is good. Because pesantren lately entered or even became an alternative education model amid the stuffy Indonesian education system and model that always reaps criticism. That is, pesantren is no longer limited to the identity of a particular group, but rather belongs to all Muslims. The popularity of pesantren is also accompanied by the publication of books discussing boarding schools. Not only written by Indonesian experts, but also foreign writers and researchers. It is not wrong that pesantren is identified as an Islamic educational institution that has a formidable power.[26]

Through its long history, this institution can still survive and even show its true strength.

II. 7. 1. Challenges and Demands of Human Resources Development

Facing the global world as it is today, where employment requires technological capability and

---

[26] Prof. DR. H. Imama Suprayogo, *Loc. Cit*, http://rektor.uin-malang.ac.id/index.php/artikel/439-21-07-2008.html

professionalism is natural when the attention of experts and observers is directed at the world of boarding schools. The fundamental thing that needs to be put forward in this context is how does pesantren adapt to the demands of such times? If what is needed is the power of religious knowledge that gives birth to morality and ketaqwaan, then obviously pesantren alumni have an advantage. However, if what is needed is a professional worker with science and technology skills then the fundamental question is worth asking in the world of pesantren.

Without intending apology let alone defending pesantren, the atmosphere of "gelagapan" facing the demands of today is experienced not only by pesantren, but also by public schools and universities. If the unemployed in this country are increasingly bloated, presumpose not only (only) from pesantren but many come from modern educational institutions. "Strangely enough," is precisely enough unemployed to come from scholars. This is reality. Although this is kasuistic, it needs special attention and serious effort towards more meaningful improvement. I am quite "concerned" and "proud" to have met an agricultural entrepreneur who does not have a diploma, it turns out that his employees are partly graduates of the Faculty of Agriculture. Not the other way around, agricultural graduates employ alumni of boarding schools. Seeing this phenomenon I became proud, it turns out that pesantren graduates are able to lead various economic efforts. Another example, in the broader sphere, not a few alumni of boarding schools become politicians, successful entrepreneurs, and successfully achieve strategic positions among the public. Dr. H. Hidayat Nur Wahid, MA., chairman of MPR RI, is an alumnus of Pesantren Modern Gontor. The victory of the political parties PKB, PAN, PKB, and PPP is a representation of the political victory of the students. Not a few kyai and students of pesantren alumni occupy strategic positions in this republic, such as the regent / mayor and the chairman of the DPRD. National figures such as Prof. Dr. M. Din Syamsuddin, Prof. Dr. Amin Abdullah, Prof. Dr. Komaruddin Hidayat, Prof. Dr. Qodri Azizy, (alm), Prof.Dr.Tholkhah Hasan, Dr Tholkhah Mansyur (alm), and many others are to receive boarding school education.

In addition, education should be distinguished from just course institutions. Educational institutions, let alone universities, should be able to deliver students to be intelligent, and not just skilled. Educational institutions should not be reduced to institutions oriented solely towards technically skilled human development, but dry and mushy of intelligence. Boarding school education, one of the more points, is being able to portray itself as an educational institution that educates it. Therefore, in the future, not only pesantren but also modern educational institutions need to be restored to their strategic position, which is to bring students to be intelligent and noble, in addition to being skilled.

Adapting pesantren with global developments full of science and technology content is not too difficult. Because pesantren has a high adaptive power. The development of pesanren by opening public education programs, such as public schools in pesantren, boarding schools, boarding school entrance skills, courses and so on is a way of boarding school in adapting to the challenges and demands of the outside world. The results are quite interesting. In some places, pesantren also organizes excellent schools and certain professions that the community needs. The problem facing pesantren is related to the nature of its independence. There has never been a boarding school where teachers, funding and support are waiting to be helped by the government. And no boarding school gets DIPA as much as government educational institutions in general. And without it, it turns out that some pesantren can survive. Therefore, if pesantren is expected to move forward together, then it needs to be applied equally, at least assisted in meeting its needs.

Pesantren, which has not yet developed new programs, --public schools, not least managed to get its students into important roles in the community. What pesantren needs today is recognition by formal educational institutions, including by the government. The obstacles that are often faced by them, because they do not hold a diploma, the knowledge gained from pesantren is not recognized. The problem with pesantren alumni is formalization. However, for most pesantren it is not actually considered a problem, because as stated in advance, pesantren is not oriented to achieve something just that is formal. Indeed, by ignoring the formal, the problem faced is when alumni enter formal sectors, such as when they run for the legislature or executive, companies that recruit workers by requiring diplomas and others. Alumni of boarding schools that successfully enter the formal sectors, are those who obtain diplomas through equality or are double educated, schools as well as pay in pesantren. It's just that not all boarding school students go to double education like this.

II.7.2. **Pondok Pesantren Answers the Challenges of Modernization.**

Today boarding schools have become the center of all forms of Muslim life. Not only has it become a place of learning, but more than that the boarding school has developed into a center of economic, political, social and community empowerment. As a social institution, pesantren has answered the need for cheap and quality education. At the same time accommodate students from all walks of life without discriminating against the socioeconomic level of parents.

This does not happen automatically, but efforts over a long period of time so that pesantren can prove itself as a surviving educational institution and have a high level of integrity in society as well as being a moral reference to the life of the general public.

The number of boarding schools in Indonesia is not less than 17,000. With a large amount, it is logical that the donation of boarding schools to the dynamics of nationality is very significant. Even before the "NKRI" State of the Unitary State of the Republic of Indonesia was formed, boarding schools had become the vanguard for the birth of the nation's fighters who defended the dignity and dignity of the Indonesian people. After the independence of pesantren contribution continues to this day.

Education figures such as Dr. Soebardi and Prof. Jhons (1982) when asked about educational institutions that are ideal for the development of indonesian characters and characters, without hesitation both agreed on pesantren as an answer. Similarly, the development of excellent schools such as Sma Taruna Nusantara and other flagship schools scattered throughout Indonesia always take pesantren as a prototype in building the brilliance of the nation's education.

This is a clear proof that the existence of boarding schools is a form of modernization that is a conscious choice of the Indonesian nation. Alberto Guerreiro Ramos (1980) stated that every nation has the right to choose and determine its own national development model, including the national education system. The modernization pattern imitated from other nations is only possible if there are no possibilities of modernization itself. Thus pesantren has become the answer to modernization for the Nation ofIndonesia.

Pesantren with various forms and management reveals the same common thread that provides one factor that seeks to benefit the learning process for students. The foundation of religion is a major factor in the success of education. The drive to always deepen religious knowledge becomes a spirit factor in the journey of the wheel of the educational process. Thus the islamic education system is a valuable asset for the Nation of Indonesia. The inclusion of boarding schools in Indonsia's national education system has encouraged the synergy of education managed by the community independently.

From the description of pesantren and the importance of learning, it takes one effort and effort to conduct a continuous dialogue throughout life in understanding the basic teachings of religion then carry out implementation in the form of daily social reality life. Each activity is based, moved and directed as an educational process. This combination of belief and contextual structure will then form a plenary (perfect) view of life. The end of it all rests on a desire to perfect the faith, Islam and faith.

The public sees the times as different all the time. Therefore, it takes one whole provision to respond to the modernization of the times. In mastuhu view (1994) the existence of pesnatren has begun since 400 years ago. With a track record like this, there is a natural selection process that goes through. If it were not for the competitive advantage of pesantren in preparing its graduates to be in the middle of society, then pesantren would not last for hundreds of years.

Learning at this time is very difficult with very complex challenges. The rapid advancement of science and technology encouraged mankind into industrial society. Of course, there needs to be anticipation early on in looking at the learning process. If physically, pesantren provides a 24-hour dormitory to study, then on the next day every student despite having a "heart asarama" that resides in every soul santri that the development of science and technology always has to blend into the morals of religion as a unit applied in daily life. Thus pesantren culture learns for 24 hours a day not only when in the territory of pesantren but more broadly to the class that is in the community.

BAB III

Cover

III. 1. Conclusion

Pondok Pesantren as an Islamic educational institution that has long worked in the world of Indonesian education is very likely to be encouraged to be an ideal Islamic educational institution and the center of Indonesian Muslim civilization in the future.

Along with the development of boarding schools face complex challenges. The flow of globalization becomes a challenge for pondok pesnatren. The rapid development of science and technology is driving humanity into industrial society. So boarding schools need to equip their students with science and technology. To be able to compete well in the midst of society and the unstoppable flow of globalization.

The development of communication and information technology is also a major challenge of boardingschools. Realizing that pesatren increase competition by using the internet as a means of communication and information. Even lately not least of pesantren who already have a website or blog on the internet. At the very least this will be a tool to mobilize the ideas and ideas of pesantren academics into the wider community without being limited by space and time.

In order to lead to the mastery of science and technology, both communication and information leading to the mastery of pesantren network needs to be considered several things. *First, an* open attitude towards change. Attitude openness will be the initial capital of building awareness of cultural learning and progress achieved by others. *Second, freedom* of thought. During this time, santri was described as a gloved people full of cheesemudan and blind taqlids had to be changed. The understanding that learning other than religion will not get reward should be changed, replaced by the understanding that building a better life in the world with the mastery of the internet network is part of God's command SWT as caliph fi ardl (manager of God). Because if the internet network is not controlled by pesantren in this case the students. Then the internet network will be controlled by parties or people who are not responsible for negative and damaging things. With the mastery of the internet network students are able to create islamic websites or blogs. If students are able to create Islamic websites or blogs then it will be the penetration of the spread of porn sites and uneducated on the Internet.

We can imagine if all students in Indonesia who number approximately two million can and can create islamic blogs or websites. The devastating results will greatly improve the rating of Islamic sites and blogs on the Internet, this will be penetration and bomerang for porn sites.

Pondok pesantren has been tested since a long time ago able to survive in the midst of modernization, because it has a high custom in addition to its popular and societal educationsystem. Many elements that can make boarding school able to become an ideal Islamic educational institution and the center of Muslim civilization in the future include:

1. **The principle of the establishment of Boarding**School.

    Boarding school was born and grew out of the calling of the heart and soul of its founder. So that in its management is done with sincerity and responsibility so that obstacles and obstacles can be passed.

2. **Orientation of Boarding School.**

    The education and teaching system developed in Pondok pesantren is oriented towards the community based education, so that boarding schools are easy to accept and close to the hearts of the community. So boarding schools are able to grow rapidly. Besides, the cottage is also oriented towards muslimism and scientific. So boarding schools foster and educate thoroughly.

3. **Boarding School as a Formal Education Complement.**

Real educational values are more likely to be implemented in boarding schools than formal school environments. Because the components and elements of education are integrated in one educational environment.

4. **Consistency and Keistiqamahan.**

The consistency and keistiqamahan boarding school has been tested in playing its role in the world of education, hal this is due to several factors::

   a. Pondok Pesantren has value and soul.

   b. Boarding school is a boarding school.

   c. Pondok Pesantren's integrated curriculum, which teaches religious science and kawniyah science

5. **Has Characteristics and Characteristics.**

Modern boarding schools have characteristics and characteristics that can be seen from several aspects including the following:

   a. Institutional (Diwakafkan)

   b. Education System (combining boarding school system with dormitory, pattern of planting values of diversity and mental attitude formation).

    c. Curriculum (teaching religious science and general science).

    d. Learning System (classical system)

    e. Learning Methods (including dialogue, q&A, discussions, demonstrations, exercises, assignments).

    f. Infrastructure (complete infrastructure such as mosques, dormitories, libraries, study rooms, laboratories, teacher housing, offices, auditoriums, business units, and sports facilities).

6. **Boarding schools have a high adaptability so that they are quick in responding to changes.**

7. **Pondok pesantren is an ideal educational institution for the development of indonesian characters and characters (Dr. Soebardi and Prof. Jhons).** This is evident by the emergence of flagship schools throughout Indonesia taking pesantren as a prototype in building the brilliance of education.

8. **Pesantren has a competitive advantage in preparing its graduates to be in the middle of society (Mastuhu).** This is seen from the track record of boarding schools since 400 years ago still exists to the day.

III. 2. SARAN

Based on this paper, the suggestions that can be put forward are as follows:

1. The attention of the government, the Ministry of Religion and all parties to the development and survival of boarding schools that have not been independent (in the development stage) in order to continue to be improved. So is the advanced boarding school.

2. To give recognition to the alumni of boarding schools, especially the recognition of the national community. Equality of boarding school diplomas with public schools or vocational schools.

3. Support for boarding schools from all parties is indispensable, both material and moril support for the future development of boarding schools, so that pesantren continues to grow.

4. Pondok pesantren needs to continue to improve itself to improve its quality in various aspects so that it creates an ideal Islamic educational institution and becomes the center of Indonesian Muslim civilization in the future.

5. The development and changes that occur in boarding schools should not deviate from the khithahnya, do

not change the values and orientation of education that exist in pondok pesatren.

6. Develop the educational curriculum of boarding schools in accordance with the development and demands of the era without changing orientation and eliminating its identity.
7. Empowering boarding schools as the driving force of the community economy.

Bibliography

Zarkasyi, Abdullah Syukri. 2005. *Gontor and Pesantren Education*Renewal. First Print, Jakarta: PT. RajaGrafindo Persada.

Zarkasyi, Abdullah Syukri. 2005. *Pesantren Management Modern Gontor Cottage*Experience. Second print, Ponorogo: Trimurti Press.

_______, 1996. *Biography of K.H. Imam Zarkasyi From Gontor Pioneering Modern Pesantren*. First Print, Ponorogo: Gontor Press.

_______, 2007. *Management of KMI Pondok Modern Darussalam Gontor*. Second Edition, Ponorogo: Darussalam Press.

_______, 2007. *Thesis Writing*Guidelines. The second print, The Institute of Research and Scientific Studies of the Institute of Islamic Studies Darussalam.

Zarkasyi, Imam. 2010. *Introductory Week of Pondok Modern Darussalam Gontor*. Ponorogo: Darussalam Press.

Zarkasyi, Imam. 2010.*A Brief Overview of Pondok Modern Darussalam Gontor*. Ponorogo: Darusslam Press.

Aly, Abdullah and Mustafa. 1998. History *of Indonesian Islamic Education.* First print, Bandung: CV. Loyal Library.

Shobahussurur. 2006. "Islamic Educational Institute in ClassicalTreasures: Study the Process of History and Transmission of Science" Lembaga Pendidikan Islam dalam Khazanah Klasik *Tsaqafah Journal of Islamic Science and*Culture. (Volume 2, Number 2, 2006/1427) p. 13. 251-273.

Abdullah, Taufik. 1987. Islam *and Society: Reflections of Indonesian*History. Jakarta: LP3ES.

Arifin, Imran. 1991. *Kyai Leadership: The Case of Tebuireng Boarding*School. Jombang: Kalimasada Press.

Arifin. M. 1987. *Philosophy of Islamic Education.* Jakarta: Bina Aksara.

Hezbollah. 1999. History *of Islamic Education in Indonesia: The Historical Trajectory of Growth and Development.* Jakarta: King Grafindo Persada.

Mastuhu. 1994. *Dinamika Sistem Pendidikan Pesantren*. Jakarta: INIS.

Dhofier, Zamakhsyari. Pesantren Tradition: The Study of Kyai's Life View. Jakarta: LP3ES.

Suprayogo, Imam. *"Pesantren and Future Education Format"*. http://rektor.uin-malang.ac.id/index.php/artikel/439-21-07-2008.html

————, *"Boarding School between Modernization and Maintaining Khitoh"* http://www.stail.ac.id/index.php?option=com_content&view=article&id=177:pondok-pesantren-antara-modernisasi-dan-mempertahankan-khittah&catid=45:jurnal-mahasiswa..

HS Barudin. *"Reform and Modernization of Islamic Education in Indonesia"*. http://www.pmiicamar.com/index.php?option=com_content&view=article&id=81:reformasi-dan-modernisasi-pendidikan-islam-di-indonesia-perspektif-dunia-pestrend.

————, *"Revitalization of Pesantren Strategic Role Republic"*http://fransiscuswelirang.com

Abdullah Badri, Muhammad. *"The Future Challenge of Pesantren"* (Republika, Friday, July 11, 2008).

S. Wekke, Ismail. *"Islamic Tradition, Model of Learning Wisdom of Life."* (http://www.pewarta-kabarinindonesia.blogspot.com, 31 August 2008).

Manfred, Ziemek. 1986. *Pesantren in Social Change.* Jakarta: P3M.